PowerXL Smokeless Grill Cookbook for Beginners

Easy and Delicious Recipes for Smart People to
Master Your Smokeless Indoor Grill

Byron J. Torres

Table of Content

Introduction

Being a great lover of grilling indoors, I had always wanted a more effective way to grill my barbecue, bacon, and other meals I love. While traditional grilling methods get the job done, they come with smokes and inconsistencies that make grilling less convenient. However, my discovery of the Power XL Smokeless Grill was a huge relief for me because with it, I get to enjoy a smoke-free grilling with evenly cooked meals right in my kitchen.

However, there were specific challenges I encountered while using the Power XL Smokeless Grill that I wished I had found easy ways to troubleshoot, and there were some mistakes I made that could have been avoided if I had some basic, adequate knowledge right before I started using my Power XL Smokeless Grill. This is why I decided to write this book to help people currently in the same positions I was in when I first purchased my Power XL Smokeless Grill by providing helpful insights and tips when using the Power XL Smokeless Grill.

In this book, I will share my experience with the Power XL Smokeless Grill, explain its features and benefits in detail so you can fully make the most of your Power XL Smokeless Grill functions. I will also be sharing tips and hints on using the Power XL Smokeless Grill in the best way possible. You will find answers to your most frequently asked questions to troubleshoot specific challenges when they occur, and you will find creative recipes to spice up your cooking routine when using the Power XL Smokeless Grill.

Below are the different recipes you will find in this book:

- Poultry Recipes
- Fish and Seafood Recipes
- Beef, Pork and Lamb Recipes
- Bread and Sandwiches
- Snack and Dessert Recipes

Let's get started.

Chapter 1: PowerXl Smokeless Grill

The Power XL Smokeless Grill is a functional kitchen smokeless grill that allows you to make delicious barbecues from the comfort of your home. It is equipped with AirFlow technology with a smoke-capture fan that removes the hot and smoky air that comes from grilling. The Power XL Smokeless Grill practically soaks in the smoke and brings back clean and fresh air into your home while you grill.

As a barbecue lover who loves to prepare my favorite barbecue without firing up the grill, my Power XL Smokeless Grill comes in handy. With this particular cooking appliance, I can cook safely in my home without worrying about impeding my health with excess smoke or disturbing my neighbors. I can make my favorite dishes safely and conveniently, right from the comfort of my home.

I love preparing safe and healthy meals, so I stay away from excess fat and oil whenever I can. Thankfully, my Power XL Smokeless Grill has been great at helping me stay true to my goal because, with my Power XL Smokeless Grill, I can prepare my favorite meals and keep excess fat and oil to the minimum. Unlike traditional cooking methods that come with inconsistencies due to fluctuating heat control, my Power XL Smokeless Grill produces consistent results all year round for every type of meals. My meals never get overcooked or undercooked, unless, of course, I want them to be.

How Does the Power XL Grill Work?

The Power XL Smokeless Grill comes with a non-stick cooking surface, a non-stick grill plate, heating element, glass lid, electric fan, and a fan cover base. The grilling is done through advanced infrared heating technology for efficient grilling. This feature is what helps cook the meals evenly, without a side getting overdone than the other. The best part? I get superb evenly cooking while keeping the heat emission to the barest minimum.

The Power XL Smokeless Grill minimizes the amount of oil that splatters while I grill. Instead of splashing when the oil drops on a hot surface, the Power XL Smokeless Grill comes with a drip tray that captures the oil, so the oil falls safely into it, thereby preventing smoke. The truth is, my steak and bacon emit smoke naturally, but the smoke is captured by the Power XL Smokeless Grill n-abduction fan.

The Power XL Smokeless Grill enables me to cook my meals faster than I would with the traditional cooking methods, and the fact that I can get so much with so little oil is a significant highlight for me. In the next chapter, I will be walking you through the different parts of the Power XL Smokeless Grill and the numerous benefits the Power XL Smokeless Grill has to offer.

Power XL Smokeless Grill Parts and Features

The Power XL Smokeless Grill is a highly phenomenal tool that comes with several unique benefits. The fantastic benefits of the Power XL Smokeless Grill are made possible through the features it is equipped with. In this chapter, I will be discussing the essential parts and features of the Power XL Smokeless Grill so you will be able to fully maximize the full opportunities that the Power XL Smokeless Grill has to offer.

Parts and Features

1. *Airflow Technology*

The Power XL Smokeless Grill comes with an Airflow Technology that takes in smoke while I'm grilling. It doesn't stop at that, it eliminates this smoke and filters in clean air into my home. This way, I can cook without having to combat smoke while I make my favorite barbecue, bacon, and other fantastic meals I enjoy.

2. *Non-Stick Cross-Hatch Grill Plate*

The Power XL Smokeless Grill is equipped with a non-stick Cross-Hatch Grill Plate that gives me the diamond-shaped grill marks I love. With the Power XL Smokeless Grill, I can make unique restaurant-style diamond-shaped grills right from my home. What's more? The non-stick Power XL Smokeless Grill means I don't have to use much oil to grill my foods. With little or no oil, my meals are perfect to go. The non-stick grill plate is dishwasher safe, so cleaning and maintenance are a breeze. I only have to detach it from my grill and put it in my dishwasher for cleaning after cooking.

3. *Non-Stick Griddle Plate*

The Power XL Smokeless Grill non-sticking cooking surface is multi-use. This enables me to make the perfect pancakes, bacon, eggs, and sandwiches just how I like them. The griddle plate is also great for producing juicy, tasty, and perfectly seared meals that delight.

4. *Large Cooking Surface*

The Power XL Smokeless Grill has a large cooking surface that accommodates a large chunk of foods. This feature has been handy for days I cook for a large number of people. I can load large sizes of steaks, veggies, and bacon and get them grilled in minutes. I rarely have to cook in batches due to the ample cooking space the Power XL Smokeless grill offers. This means I don't have to wait for long before I relish my meals.

5. **Drip Tray**

The Power XL drip tray is perfect for collecting oils, grease, and excess fat that comes from my grilled meals. This Drip tray offers two significant advantages. First, it contributes to reducing the smoke associated with grilling. This is because rather than drop on a hot surface to produce smoke, the oil flows directly into the drip tray, which helps eliminate smoke. Secondly, the drip tray ensures the grill and grilling environment is mess-free because rather than the grease and oil splattering around the grill, they go into the drip tray. So, after I'm done grilling, I only have to remove the drip tray and wash off the grease and oil in the dishwasher.

6. *Glass Lid*

The Power XL Smokeless Grill comes with a tempered glass lid that offers the excellent seal feature whenever I cook my food. The efficient glass lids keep the air locked inside to make cooking faster. This also helps to keep my meals tasty because the flavor and steam have no chance of escape. They, therefore, get soaked into my food to come juicy, flavored, and deliciously tasty.

Power XL Smokeless Grill Hints and Maintenance Tricks

The Power XL Smokeless Grill is a highly durable, functional kitchen tool that can work all year round without a hitch. However, knowing some maintenance tips would help you make the best use of your Power XL Smokeless Grill to serve you better. Let's discuss some insider hints and tricks of the Power XL Smokeless Grill in this chapter.

1. One of the essential things I do when I use the Power XL Smokeless Grill is to use separate utensils. I use different utensils for both my raw meals and the grilled meat to avoid the transfer of germs.

2. It always helps to partially cook your bone-in chicken, smoked fish, or fresh sausages before you grill with the Power XL Smokeless Grill. I've discovered from experience that if the chicken or ribs aren't partially cooked before you grill, my steaks, chicken, and fish get overly brown without being adequately cooked on the inside. To achieve the best results with grilling, I recommend you partially cook your meats before you grill.

3. Another helpful thing is to ensure not to use metallic utensils when you use the Power XL Smokeless Grill. Using metallic utensils puts your Power XL Smokeless grill cooking surface at the risk of scratches. Ensure to keep your grill away from metallic utensils to preserve its appearance.

4. Another thing to avoid is chopping, cutting, and slicing on the Power XL Smokeless Grill cooking surface. If you do, then you may likely scratch the surface of your cooking grill over time.

5. Avoid using coarse materials like steel wool to clean your Power XL Smokeless Grill, especially the surface. Cleaning the surface of your Power XL Smokeless Grill with steel wool can cause scratches on the surface.

FAQs on Power XL Smokeless Grill

In this chapter, I will be answering some common questions you may have when using the Power XL Smokeless Grill. These questions will come in handy whenever you encounter some common challenges with the Power XL Smokeless Grill. Let's dive in.

1. *Is the Power XL Smokeless Grill easy to clean?*

Cleaning and maintaining my Power XL Smokeless grill is almost effortless. The grill and griddle plate, drip tray, and lid are all dishwasher safe and do not require hand washing unless you want to. I recommend you to clean the base unit with a warm and damp cloth with a bit of liquid. If you have to clean the heating unit, ensure you don't do so immediately after cooking. Unplug the grill first and allow it to cool down completely. After this, use a damp cloth to clean.

2. How much can I cook with the Power XL Smokeless Grill?

The Power XL smokeless grill has a large cooking surface. It can grill about six burgers and four steaks simultaneously. This enables you to cook as much as you want for yourself and your family.

3. How do I control the cooking temperature of my Power XL Smokeless Grill?

The power XL Smokeless grill comes with a LED intelligent temperature control that enables you to adjust your grill. You can change the temperature just by clicking a button on your grill.

4. Does the Power XL Smokeless Grill offer a grilled flavor or smoky taste?

Yes, the Power XL Smokeless Grill does offer a grilled flavor and smoky taste. It helps retain the flavor and taste of your grill through the glass lid. You will get the same flavor and texture an outdoor grill will provide.

5. How do I get my Power XL Smokeless Grill to cook and heat up evenly?

To ensure my Power XL Smokeless Grill properly heats up to cook evenly, I ensure to assemble my grill correctly, placing the arrow marked on the drip pan towards the heating element. If you don't assemble the Drip pan correctly, it can affect the heating element and cause it not to work.

Chapter 2 Breakfasts

Bacon and Egg Bread Cups

Prep time: 10 minutes | Cook time: 8 to 12 minutes | Serves 4

4 (3-by-4-inch) crusty rolls

4 thin slices Gouda or Swiss cheese mini wedges

5 eggs

2 tablespoons heavy cream

3 strips precooked bacon, chopped

½ teaspoon dried thyme

Pinch salt

Freshly ground black pepper, to taste

1. On a clean work surface, cut the tops off the rolls. Using your fingers, remove the insides of the rolls to make bread cups, leaving a ½-inch shell. Place a slice of cheese onto each roll bottom. 2. Whisk together the eggs and heavy cream in a medium bowl until well combined. Fold in the bacon, thyme, salt, and pepper and stir well. 3. Scrape the egg mixture into the prepared bread cups. 4. Add about 2 cups water to the water tray. 5. Press the Power button on the Power Smokeless Grill XL, and set the grill temperature to 320°F (160°C). Allow the grill to preheat for 5 minutes. 6. Once preheated, place the bread cups over the grill plate. Press the Fan button to engage the fan. Close the glass lid and bake for 8 to 12 minutes, or until the eggs are cooked to your preference. 7. Serve warm.

Apple and Walnut Muffins

Prep time: 15 minutes | Cook time: 10 minutes | Makes 8 muffins

1 cup flour

⅓ cup sugar

1 teaspoon baking powder

¼ teaspoon baking soda

¼ teaspoon salt

1 teaspoon cinnamon

¼ teaspoon ginger

¼ teaspoon nutmeg

1 egg

2 tablespoons pancake syrup, plus 2 teaspoons

2 tablespoons melted butter, plus 2 teaspoons

¾ cup unsweetened applesauce

½ teaspoon vanilla extract

¼ cup chopped walnuts

¼ cup diced apple

1. In a large bowl, stir together the flour, sugar, baking powder, baking soda, salt, cinnamon, ginger, and nutmeg. 2. In a small bowl, beat egg until frothy. Add syrup, butter, applesauce, and vanilla and mix well. 3. Pour egg mixture into dry ingredients and stir just until moistened. 4. Gently stir in nuts and diced apple. 5. Divide batter among 8 parchment paper-lined muffin cups. 6. Add about 2 cups water to the water tray. 7. Press the Power button on the Power Smokeless Grill XL, and set the grill temperature to 320°F (160°C). Allow the grill to preheat for 5 minutes. 8. Once

preheated, put 4 muffin cups over the grill plate. Press the Fan button to engage the fan. Close the glass lid and bake for 10 minutes. 9. Repeat with remaining 4 muffins or until toothpick inserted in center comes out clean. 9. Serve warm.

Ham and Corn Muffins

Prep time: 10 minutes | Cook time: 6 minutes | Makes 8 muffins

1 cup flour

⅓ cup sugar

1 teaspoon baking powder

¾ cup yellow cornmeal

¼ cup flour

1½ teaspoons baking powder

¼ teaspoon salt

1 egg, beaten

2 tablespoons canola oil

½ cup milk

½ cup shredded sharp Cheddar cheese

½ cup diced ham

1. In a medium bowl, stir together the cornmeal, flour, baking powder, and salt. 2. Add the egg, oil, and milk to dry ingredients and mix well. 3. Stir in shredded cheese and diced ham. 4. Divide batter among 8 parchment paper-lined muffin cups. 5. Add about 2 cups water to the water tray. 6. Press the Power button on the Power Smokeless Grill XL, and set the grill temperature to 390°F (199°C). Allow the grill to preheat for 5 minutes. 7. Once preheated, put 4 filled muffin cups over the grill plate. Press the Fan button to engage the fan. Close the glass lid and bake for 5 minutes. 8. Reduce temperature to 320 °F (160°C) and bake for 1 minute or until a toothpick inserted in center of the muffin comes out clean. 9. Repeat steps 7 and 8 to bake remaining muffins. 10. Serve warm.

Soufflé

Prep time: 10 minutes | Cook time: 22 minutes | Serves 4

⅓ cup butter, melted

¼ cup flour

1 cup milk

1 ounce (28 g) sugar

4 egg yolks

1 teaspoon vanilla extract

6 egg whites

1 teaspoon cream of tartar

Cooking spray

1. In a bowl, mix the butter and flour until a smooth consistency is achieved. 2. Pour the milk into a saucepan over medium-low heat. Add the sugar and allow to dissolve before raising the heat to boil the milk. 3. Pour in the flour and butter mixture and stir rigorously for 7 minutes to eliminate any lumps. Make sure the mixture thickens. Take off the heat and allow to cool for 15 minutes. 4. Add about 2 cups water to the water tray. Press the Power button on the Power Smokeless Grill XL, and set the grill temperature to 320°F (160°C). Allow the grill to preheat for 5 minutes. 5. Spritz 6 soufflé dishes with cooking spray. 6. Put the egg yolks and vanilla extract in a separate bowl and beat them together with a fork. Pour in the milk and combine well to incorporate everything. 7. In a smaller bowl mix the egg whites and cream of tartar with a fork. Fold into the egg yolks-milk mixture before adding in the flour mixture. Transfer equal amounts to the 6 soufflé dishes. 8. Once preheated, put the dishes in the grill. Press the Fan button to engage the fan. Close the glass lid and bake for 15 minutes. 9. Serve warm.

Tomato-Corn Frittata with Avocado Dressing

Prep time: 10 minutes | Cook time: 20 minutes | Serves 2 or 3

½ cup cherry tomatoes, halved

Kosher salt and freshly ground black pepper, to taste

6 large eggs, lightly beaten

½ cup corn kernels, thawed if frozen

¼ cup milk

1 tablespoon finely chopped fresh dill

½ cup shredded Monterey Jack cheese

Avocado Dressing:

1 ripe avocado, pitted and peeled

2 tablespoons fresh lime juice

¼ cup olive oil

1 scallion, finely chopped

8 fresh basil leaves, finely chopped

1. Put the tomato halves in a colander and lightly season with salt. Set aside for 10 minutes to drain well. Pour the tomatoes into a large bowl and fold in the eggs, corn, milk, and dill. Sprinkle with salt and pepper and stir until mixed. 2. Add about 2 cups water to the water tray. Press the Power button on the Power Smokeless Grill XL, and set the grill temperature to 320°F (160°C). Allow the grill to preheat for 5 minutes. 3. Once preheated, pour the egg mixture into a baking pan. Place the pan directly over the grill plate. Press the Fan button to engage the fan. Close the glass lid and bake for 15 minutes. 4. Scatter the cheese on top. Continue to cook for another 5 minutes, or until the frittata is puffy and set. 5. Meanwhile, make the avocado dressing: Mash the avocado with the lime juice in a medium bowl until smooth. Mix in the olive oil, scallion, and

basil and stir until well incorporated. 6. Let the frittata cool for 5 minutes and serve alongside the avocado dressing.

Breakfast Tater Tot Casserole

Prep time: 5 minutes | Cook time: 17 to 19 minutes | Serves 4

4 eggs

1 cup milk

Salt and pepper, to taste

12 ounces (340 g) ground chicken sausage

1 pound (454 g) frozen tater tots, thawed

¾ cup grated Cheddar cheese

Cooking spray

1. Whisk together the eggs and milk in a medium bowl. Season with salt and pepper to taste and stir until mixed. Set aside. 2. Place a skillet over medium-high heat and spritz with cooking spray. Place the ground sausage in the skillet and break it into smaller pieces with a spatula or spoon. Cook for 3 to 4 minutes until the sausage starts to brown, stirring occasionally. Remove from heat and set aside. 3. Add about 2 cups water to the water tray. Press the Power button on the Power Smokeless Grill XL, and set the grill temperature to 390°F (199°C). Allow the grill to preheat for 5 minutes. 4. Coat a baking pan with cooking spray. 5. Arrange the tater tots in the baking pan. Once preheated, place the pan directly over the grill plate. Press the Fan button to engage the fan. Close the glass lid and bake for 15 minutes. Stir in the egg mixture and cooked sausage. Bake for another 6 minutes. 6. Scatter the cheese on top of the tater tots. Continue to bake for 2 to 3 minutes more until the cheese is bubbly and melted. 7. Let the mixture cool for 5 minutes and serve warm.

Chocolate Banana Bread with White Chocolate

Prep time: 10 minutes | Cook time: 30 minutes | Serves 4

¼ cup cocoa powder

6 tablespoons plus 2 teaspoons all-purpose flour, divided

½ teaspoon kosher salt

¼ teaspoon baking soda

1½ ripe bananas

1 large egg, whisked

¼ cup vegetable oil

½ cup sugar

3 tablespoons buttermilk or plain yogurt (not Greek)

½ teaspoon vanilla extract

6 tablespoons chopped white chocolate

6 tablespoons chopped walnuts

1. Add about 2 cups water to the water tray. Press the Power button on the Power Smokeless Grill XL, and set the grill temperature to 320°F (160°C). Allow the grill to preheat for 5 minutes. 2. Mix together the cocoa powder, 6 tablespoons of the flour, salt, and baking soda in a medium bowl. 3. Mash the bananas with a fork in another medium bowl until smooth. Fold in the egg, oil, sugar, buttermilk, and vanilla, and whisk until thoroughly combined. Add the wet mixture to the dry mixture and stir until well incorporated. 4. Combine the white chocolate, walnuts, and the remaining 2 tablespoons of flour in a third bowl and toss to coat. Add this mixture to the batter and stir until well incorporated. Pour the batter into a baking pan and smooth the top with a spatula. 5. Once preheated, place the pan directly over the grill plate. Press the Fan button to engage the fan. Close the glass lid and bake for 30 minutes. Check the bread for

doneness: If a toothpick inserted into the center of the bread comes out clean, it's done.

6. Remove from the grill and allow to cool on a wire rack for 10 minutes before serving.

Chapter 3 Snacks and Appetizers

Cayenne Sesame Nut Mix

Prep time: 10 minutes | Cook time: 2 minutes | Makes 4 cups

1 tablespoon buttery spread, melted

2 teaspoons honey

¼ teaspoon cayenne pepper

2 teaspoons sesame seeds

¼ teaspoon kosher salt

¼ teaspoon freshly ground black pepper

1 cup cashews

1 cup almonds

1 cup mini pretzels

1 cup rice squares cereal

Cooking spray

1. Add about 2 cups water to the water tray. Press the Power button on the Power Smokeless Grill XL, and set the grill temperature to 350°F (180°C). Allow the grill to preheat for 5 minutes. 2. In a large bowl, combine the buttery spread, honey, cayenne pepper, sesame seeds, kosher salt, and black pepper, then add the cashews, almonds, pretzels, and rice squares, tossing to coat. 3. Spray a baking pan with cooking spray, then pour the mixture into the pan. Once preheated, place the pan directly over the grill plate. Press the Fan button to engage the fan. Close the glass lid and bake for 2 minutes. 4. Remove the sesame mix from the grill and allow to cool in the pan on a wire rack for 5 minutes before serving.

Garlicky and Lemony Artichokes

Prep time: 10 minutes | Cook time: 10 minutes | Serves 4

juice of ½ lemon

½ cup canola oil

3 garlic cloves, chopped

sea salt, to taste

freshly ground black pepper, to taste

2 large artichokes, trimmed and halved

1. Add about 2 cups water to the water tray. Press the Power button on the Power Smokeless Grill XL, and set the grill temperature to 350°F (180°C). Allow the grill to preheat for 5 minutes. 2. While the unit is preheating, in a medium bowl, combine the lemon juice, oil, and garlic. season with salt and pepper, then brush the artichoke halves with the lemon-garlic mixture. 3. Once preheated, place the artichokes over the grill plate, cut side down. Gently press them down to maximize grill marks. Press the Fan button to engage the fan. Close the glass lid and bake for 8 to 10 minutes, occasionally basting generously with the lemon-garlic mixture throughout cooking, until blistered on all sides.

Zucchini and Potato Tots

Prep time: 5 minutes | Cook time: 20 minutes | Serves 4

1 large zucchini, grated

1 medium baked potato, skin removed and mashed

¼ cup shredded Cheddar cheese

1 large egg, beaten

½ teaspoon kosher salt

Cooking spray

1. Add about 2 cups water to the water tray. Press the Power button on the Power Smokeless Grill XL, and set the grill temperature to 390°F (199°C). Allow the grill to preheat for 5 minutes. 2. Wrap the grated zucchini in a paper towel and squeeze out any excess liquid, then combine the zucchini, baked potato, shredded Cheddar cheese, egg, and kosher salt in a large bowl. 3. Spray a baking pan with cooking spray, then place individual tablespoons of the zucchini mixture in the pan. Once preheated, place the pan directly over the grill plate. Press the Fan button to engage the fan. Close the glass lid and grill for 10 minutes. Repeat this process with the remaining mixture. 4. Remove the tots and allow to cool on a wire rack for 5 minutes before serving.

Mushroom and Spinach Calzones

Prep time: 15 minutes | Cook time: 26 to 27 minutes | Serves 4

2 tablespoons olive oil

1 onion, chopped

2 garlic cloves, minced

¼ cup chopped mushrooms

1 pound (454 g) spinach, chopped

1 tablespoon Italian seasoning

½ teaspoon oregano

Salt and black pepper, to taste

1½ cups marinara sauce

1 cup ricotta cheese, crumbled

1 (13-ounce / 369-g) pizza crust

Cooking spray

Make the Filling: 1. Heat the olive oil in a pan over medium heat until shimmering. 2. Add the onion, garlic, and mushrooms and sauté for 4 minutes, or until softened. 3. Stir in the spinach and sauté for 2 to 3 minutes, or until the spinach is wilted. Sprinkle with the Italian seasoning, oregano, salt, and pepper and mix well. 4. Add the marinara sauce and cook for about 5 minutes, stirring occasionally, or until the sauce is thickened. 5. Remove the pan from the heat and stir in the ricotta cheese. Set aside. **Make the Calzones:** 6. Spritz the grill plate with cooking spray. 7. Add about 2 cups water to the water tray. Press the Power button on the Power Smokeless Grill XL, and set the grill temperature to 390°F (199°C). Allow the grill to preheat for 5 minutes. 8. Roll the pizza crust out with a rolling pin on a lightly floured work surface, then cut it into 4 rectangles. 9. Spoon ¼ of the filling into each rectangle and fold in half. Crimp the edges with a fork to seal. Mist them with cooking spray. 10. Once preheated, place the calzones in the grill. Press the Fan button to engage the fan. Close the glass lid and bake for 15 minutes, flipping once, or until the calzones are golden brown and crisp. 11. Transfer the calzones to a paper towel-lined plate and serve.

Cheese and Ham Stuffed Baby Bella

Prep time: 15 minutes | Cook time: 12 minutes | Serves 8

4 ounces (113 g) Mozzarella cheese, cut into pieces

½ cup diced ham

2 green onions, chopped

2 tablespoons bread crumbs

½ teaspoon garlic powder

¼ teaspoon ground oregano

¼ teaspoon ground black pepper

1 to 2 teaspoons olive oil

16 fresh Baby Bella mushrooms, stemmed removed

1. Process the cheese, ham, green onions, bread crumbs, garlic powder, oregano, and pepper in a food processor until finely chopped. 2. With the food processor running, slowly drizzle in 1 to 2 teaspoons olive oil until a thick paste has formed. Transfer the mixture to a bowl. 3. Evenly divide the mixture into the mushroom caps and lightly press down the mixture. 4. Add about 2 cups water to the water tray. Press the Power button on the Power Smokeless Grill XL, and set the grill temperature to 390°F (199°C). Allow the grill to preheat for 5 minutes. 5. Once preheated, lay the mushrooms on the grill plate in a single layer. You'll need to work in batches to avoid overcrowding. 6. Press the Fan button to engage the fan. Close the glass lid and grill for 12 minutes until the mushrooms are lightly browned and tender. 7. Remove from the grill to a plate and repeat with the remaining mushrooms. 8. Let the mushrooms cool for 5 minutes and serve warm.

Sausage and Mushroom Empanadas

Prep time: 5 minutes | Cook time: 12 minutes | Serves 4

½ pound (227 g) Kielbasa smoked sausage, chopped

4 chopped canned mushrooms

2 tablespoons chopped onion

½ teaspoon ground cumin

¼ teaspoon paprika

Salt and black pepper, to taste

½ package puff pastry dough, at room temperature

1 egg, beaten

Cooking spray

1. Spritz the grill plate with cooking spray. 2. Add about 2 cups water to the water tray. Press the Power button on the Power Smokeless Grill XL, and set the grill temperature to 350°F (180°C). Allow the grill to preheat for 5 minutes. 3. Combine the sausage, mushrooms, onion, cumin, paprika, salt, and pepper in a bowl and stir to mix well. 4. Make the empanadas: Place the puff pastry dough on a lightly floured surface. Cut circles into the dough with a glass. Place 1 tablespoon of the sausage mixture into the center of each pastry circle. Fold each in half and pinch the edges to seal. Using a fork, crimp the edges. Brush them with the beaten egg and mist with cooking spray. 5. Once preheated, place the empanadas in the grill. Press the Fan button to engage the fan. Close the glass lid and bake for 12 minutes until golden brown. Flip the empanadas halfway through the cooking time. 6. Allow them to cool for 5 minutes and serve hot.

Cheesy Crab Toasts

Prep time: 10 minutes | Cook time: 5 minutes | Makes 15 to 18 toasts

1 (6-ounce / 170-g) can flaked crab meat, well drained

3 tablespoons light mayonnaise

¼ cup shredded Parmesan cheese

¼ cup shredded Cheddar cheese

1 teaspoon Worcestershire sauce

½ teaspoon lemon juice

1 loaf artisan bread, French bread, or baguette, cut into ⅜-inch-thick slices

1. Add about 2 cups water to the water tray. Press the Power button on the Power Smokeless Grill XL, and set the grill temperature to 350°F (180°C). Allow the grill to preheat for 5 minutes. 2. In a large bowl, stir together all the ingredients except the bread slices. 3. On a clean work surface, lay the bread slices. Spread ½ tablespoon of crab mixture onto each slice of bread. 4. Once preheated, arrange the bread slices on the grill plate in a single layer. You'll need to work in batches to avoid overcrowding. 5. Press the Fan button to engage the fan. Close the glass lid and bake for 5 minutes until the tops are lightly browned. 6. Transfer to a plate and repeat with the remaining bread slices. 7. Serve warm.

Cajun Zucchini Chips

Prep time: 5 minutes | Cook time: 15 to 16 minutes | Serves 4

2 large zucchini, cut into ⅛-inch-thick slices

2 teaspoons Cajun seasoning

Cooking spray

1. Spray the grill plate lightly with cooking spray. 2. Add about 2 cups water to the water tray. Press the Power button on the Power Smokeless Grill XL, and set the grill temperature to 390°F (199°C). Allow the grill to preheat for 5 minutes. 3. Put the zucchini slices in a medium bowl and spray them generously with cooking spray. 4. Sprinkle the Cajun seasoning over the zucchini and stir to make sure they are evenly coated with oil and seasoning. 5. Once preheated, place the slices in a single layer in the grill plate, making sure not to overcrowd. You will need to cook these in several batches. 6. Press the Fan button to engage the fan. Close the glass lid and cook for 8 minutes. Flip the slices over and cook for an additional 7 to 8 minutes, or until they are as crisp and brown as you prefer. 7. Serve immediately.

Bacon-Wrapped Dates

Prep time: 10 minutes | Cook time: 10 to 14 minutes | Serves 6

12 dates, pitted

6 slices high-quality bacon, cut in half

Cooking spray

1. Add about 2 cups water to the water tray. Press the Power button on the Power Smokeless Grill XL, and set the grill temperature to 350°F (180°C). Allow the grill to preheat for 5 minutes. 2. Wrap each date with half a bacon slice and secure with a toothpick. 3. Once preheated, spray the grill plate with cooking spray, then place 6 bacon-wrapped dates in the grill. Once preheated, place the dates over the grill plate. Press the Fan button to engage the fan. Close the glass lid and bake for 5 to 7 minutes or until the bacon is crispy. Repeat this process with the remaining dates. 4. Remove the dates and allow to cool on a wire rack for 5 minutes before serving.

Breaded Green Olives

Prep time: 5 minutes | Cook time: 8 minutes | Serves 4

1 (5½-ounce / 156-g) jar pitted green olives

½ cup all-purpose flour

Salt and pepper, to taste

½ cup bread crumbs

1 egg

Cooking spray

1. Add about 2 cups water to the water tray. Press the Power button on the Power Smokeless Grill XL, and set the grill temperature to 390°F (199°C). Allow the grill to preheat for 5 minutes. 2. Remove the olives from the jar and dry thoroughly with paper towels. 3. In a small bowl, combine the flour with salt and pepper to taste. Place the bread crumbs in another small bowl. In a third small bowl, beat the egg. 4. Spritz the grill plate with cooking spray. 5. Dip the olives in the flour, then the egg, and then the bread crumbs. 6. Once preheated, place the breaded olives on the grill. It is okay to stack them. Spray the olives with cooking spray. Press the Fan button to engage the fan. Close the glass lid and cook for 6 minutes. Flip the olives and cook for an additional 2 minutes, or until brown and crisp. 7. Cool before serving.

Chapter 4 Poultry

Potato Cheese Crusted Chicken

Prep time: 15 minutes | Cook time: 22 to 25 minutes | Serves 4

¼ cup buttermilk

1 large egg, beaten

1 cup instant potato flakes

¼ cup grated Parmesan cheese

1 teaspoon salt

½ teaspoon freshly ground black pepper

2 whole boneless, skinless chicken breasts (about 1 pound / 454 g each), halved

Cooking spray

1. Line the grill plate with parchment paper. 2. Add about 2 cups water to the water tray. Press the Power button on the Power Smokeless Grill XL, and set the grill temperature to 320°F (160°C). Allow the grill to preheat for 5 minutes. 3. In a shallow bowl, whisk the buttermilk and egg until blended. In another shallow bowl, stir together the potato flakes, cheese, salt, and pepper. 4. One at a time, dip the chicken pieces in the buttermilk mixture and the potato flake mixture, coating thoroughly. 5. Once preheated, place the coated chicken on the parchment and spritz with cooking spray. 6. Press the Fan button to engage the fan. Close the glass lid and bake for 15 minutes. Flip the chicken, spritz it with cooking spray, and bake for 7 to 10 minutes more until the outside is crispy and the inside is no longer pink. Serve immediately.

Strawberry-Glazed Turkey

Prep time: 15 minutes | Cook time: 37 minutes | Serves 2

2 pounds (907 g) turkey breast

1 tablespoon olive oil

Salt and ground black pepper, to taste

1 cup fresh strawberries

1. Add about 2 cups water to the water tray. Press the Power button on the Power Smokeless Grill XL, and set the grill temperature to 390°F (199°C). Allow the grill to preheat for 5 minutes. 2. Rub the turkey bread with olive oil on a clean work surface, then sprinkle with salt and ground black pepper. 3. Once preheated, transfer the turkey in the grill. Press the Fan button to engage the fan. Close the glass lid and cook for 30 minutes or until the internal temperature of the turkey reaches at least 165°F (74°C). Flip the turkey breast halfway through. 4. Meanwhile, put the strawberries in a food processor and pulse until smooth. 5. When the cooking of the turkey is complete, spread the puréed strawberries over the turkey. Close the glass lid and cook for 7 more minutes. 6. Serve immediately.

Easy Asian Turkey Meatballs

Prep time: 10 minutes | Cook time: 11 to 14 minutes | Serves 4

2 tablespoons peanut oil, divided

1 small onion, minced

¼ cup water chestnuts, finely chopped

½ teaspoon ground ginger

2 tablespoons low-sodium soy sauce

¼ cup panko bread crumbs

1 egg, beaten

1 pound (454 g) ground turkey

1. Press the Power button on the Power Smokeless Grill XL, and set the grill temperature to 390°F (199°C). Allow the grill to preheat for 5 minutes. 2. In a round metal pan, combine 1 tablespoon of peanut oil and onion. Once preheated, place the pan directly over the grill plate. Press the Fan button to engage the fan. Close the glass lid and cook for 1 to 2 minutes or until crisp and tender. Transfer the onion to a medium bowl. 3. Add the water chestnuts, ground ginger, soy sauce, and bread crumbs to the onion and mix well. Add egg and stir well. Mix in the ground turkey until combined. 4. Form the mixture into 1-inch meatballs. Drizzle the remaining 1 tablespoon of oil over the meatballs. Arrange the meatballs in the pan. 5. Place the pan directly over the grill plate. Close the glass lid and bake for 10 to 12 minutes, or until they are 165°F (74°C) on a meat thermometer. Rest for 5 minutes before serving.

China Spicy Turkey Thighs

Prep time: 10 minutes | Cook time: 25 minutes | Serves 6

2 pounds (907 g) turkey thighs

1 teaspoon Chinese five-spice powder

¼ teaspoon Sichuan pepper

1 teaspoon pink Himalayan salt

1 tablespoon Chinese rice vinegar

1 tablespoon mustard

1 tablespoon chili sauce

2 tablespoons soy sauce

Cooking spray

1. Spritz the grill plate with cooking spray. 2. Add about 2 cups water to the water tray. Press the Power button on the Power Smokeless Grill XL, and set the grill temperature to 350°F (180°C). Allow the grill to preheat for 5 minutes. 3. Rub the turkey thighs with five-spice powder, Sichuan pepper, and salt on a clean work surface. 4. Once preheated, put the turkey thighs in the grill and spritz with cooking spray. You may need to work in batches to avoid overcrowding. 5. Press the Fan button to engage the fan. Close the glass lid and cook for 22 minutes or until well browned. Flip the thighs at least three times during the cooking. 6. Meanwhile, heat the remaining ingredients in a saucepan over medium-high heat. Cook for 3 minutes or until the sauce is thickened and reduces to two thirds. 7. Transfer the thighs onto a plate and baste with sauce before serving.

Honey Rosemary Chicken

Prep time: 10 minutes | Cook time: 20 minutes | Serves 4

¼ cup balsamic vinegar

¼ cup honey

2 tablespoons olive oil

1 tablespoon dried rosemary leaves

1 teaspoon salt

½ teaspoon freshly ground black pepper

2 whole boneless, skinless chicken breasts (about 1 pound / 454 g each), halved

Cooking spray

1. In a large resealable bag, combine the vinegar, honey, olive oil, rosemary, salt, and pepper. Add the chicken pieces, seal the bag, and refrigerate to marinate for at least 2 hours. 2. Line the grill plate with parchment paper. 3. Add about 2 cups water to the water tray. Press the Power button on the Power Smokeless Grill XL, and set the grill temperature to 320°F (160°C). Allow the grill to preheat for 5 minutes. 4. Once preheated, remove the chicken from the marinade and place it on the parchment. Spritz with cooking spray. 5. Press the Fan button to engage the fan. Close the glass lid and bake for 10 minutes. Flip the chicken, spritz it with cooking spray, and bake for 10 minutes more until the internal temperature reaches 165°F (74°C) and the chicken is no longer pink inside. Let sit for 5 minutes before serving.

Lemon Parmesan Chicken

Prep time: 10 minutes | Cook time: 20 minutes | Serves 4

1 egg

2 tablespoons lemon juice

2 teaspoons minced garlic

½ teaspoon salt

½ teaspoon freshly ground black pepper

4 boneless, skinless chicken breasts, thin cut

Olive oil spray

½ cup whole-wheat bread crumbs

¼ cup grated Parmesan cheese

1. In a medium bowl, whisk together the egg, lemon juice, garlic, salt, and pepper. Add the chicken breasts, cover, and refrigerate for up to 1 hour. 2. In a shallow bowl, combine the bread crumbs and Parmesan cheese. 3. Spray the grill plate lightly with olive oil spray. 4. Add about 2 cups water to the water tray. Press the Power button on the Power Smokeless Grill XL, and set the grill temperature to 350°F (180°C). Allow the grill to preheat for 5 minutes. 5. Once preheated, remove the chicken breasts from the egg mixture, then dredge them in the bread crumb mixture, and place in the grill in a single layer. Lightly spray the chicken breasts with olive oil spray. You may need to cook the chicken in batches. 6. Press the Fan button to engage the fan. Close the glass lid and cook for 8 minutes. Flip the chicken over, lightly spray with olive oil spray, and cook for an additional 7 to 12 minutes, until the chicken reaches an internal temperature of 165°F (74°C). 7. Serve warm.

Turkey Stuffed Bell Peppers

Prep time: 20 minutes | Cook time: 15 minutes | Serves 4

½ pound (227 g) lean ground turkey

4 medium bell peppers

1 (15-ounce / 425-g) can black beans, drained and rinsed

1 cup shredded reduced-fat Cheddar cheese

1 cup cooked long-grain brown rice

1 cup mild salsa

1¼ teaspoons chili powder

1 teaspoon salt

½ teaspoon ground cumin

½ teaspoon freshly ground black pepper

Olive oil spray

Chopped fresh cilantro, for garnish

1. Add about 2 cups water to the water tray. Press the Power button on the Power Smokeless Grill XL, and set the grill temperature to 350°F (180°C). Allow the grill to preheat for 5 minutes. 2. In a large skillet over medium-high heat, cook the turkey, breaking it up with a spoon, until browned, about 5 minutes. Drain off any excess fat. 3. Cut about ½ inch off the tops of the peppers and then cut in half lengthwise. Remove and discard the seeds and set the peppers aside. 4. In a large bowl, combine the browned turkey, black beans, Cheddar cheese, rice, salsa, chili powder, salt, cumin, and black pepper. Spoon the mixture into the bell peppers. 5. Lightly spray the grill plate with olive oil spray. 6. Once preheated, place the stuffed peppers in the grill. Press the Fan button to engage the fan. Close the glass lid and cook for 10 to 15 minutes until heated through. 7. Garnish with cilantro and serve.

Turkey and Cauliflower Meatloaf

Prep time: 15 minutes | Cook time: 50 minutes | Serves 6

2 pounds (907 g) lean ground turkey

1⅓ cups riced cauliflower

2 large eggs, lightly beaten

¼ cup almond flour

⅔ cup chopped yellow or white onion

1 teaspoon ground dried turmeric

1 teaspoon ground cumin

1 teaspoon ground coriander

1 tablespoon minced garlic

1 teaspoon salt

1 teaspoon ground black pepper

Cooking spray

1. Spritz a loaf pan with cooking spray. 2. Add about 2 cups water to the water tray. Press the Power button on the Power Smokeless Grill XL, and set the grill temperature to 350°F (177°C). Allow the grill to preheat for 5 minutes. 3. Combine all the ingredients in a large bowl. Stir to mix well. Pour half of the mixture in the prepared loaf pan and press with a spatula to coat the bottom evenly. Spritz the mixture with cooking spray. 4. Once preheated, place the pan directly over the grill plate. Press the Fan button to engage the fan. Close the glass lid and bake for 25 minutes, or until the meat is well browned and the internal temperature reaches at least 165°F (74°C). Repeat with remaining mixture. 5. Remove the loaf pan from the grill and serve immediately.

Duck Breasts with Marmalade Balsamic Glaze

Prep time: 5 minutes | Cook time: 13 minutes | Serves 4

4 (6-ounce / 170-g) skin-on duck breasts

1 teaspoon salt

¼ cup orange marmalade

1 tablespoon white balsamic vinegar

¾ teaspoon ground black pepper

1. Add about 2 cups water to the water tray. Press the Power button on the Power Smokeless Grill XL, and set the grill temperature to 390°F (199°C). Allow the grill to preheat for 5 minutes. 2. Cut 10 slits into the skin of the duck breasts, then sprinkle with salt on both sides. 3. Once preheated, place the breasts in the grill, skin side up. Press the Fan button to engage the fan. Close the glass lid and cook for 10 minutes. 4. Meanwhile, combine the remaining ingredients in a small bowl. Stir to mix well. 5. When the cooking is complete, brush the duck skin with the marmalade mixture. Flip the breast and cook for 3 more minutes or until the skin is crispy and the breast is well browned. 6. Serve immediately.

Steak and Lettuce Salad

Prep time: 5 minutes | Cook time: 16 minutes | Serves 4 to 6

4 (8-ounce / 227-g) skirt steaks

Sea salt, to taste

Freshly ground black pepper, to taste

6 cups chopped romaine lettuce

¾ cup cherry tomatoes, halved

¼ cup blue cheese, crumbled

1 cup croutons

2 avocados, peeled and sliced

1 cup blue cheese dressing

1. Add about 2 cups water to the water tray. Press the Power button on the Power Smokeless Grill XL, and set the grill temperature to 390°F (199°C). Allow the grill to preheat for 5 minutes. 2. Season the steaks on both sides with the salt and pepper. 3. Once preheated, place 2 steaks over the grill plate. Gently press the steaks down to maximize grill marks. Press the Fan button to engage the fan. Close the glass lid and cook for 4 minutes. After 4 minutes, flip the steaks, cook for an additional 4 minutes. 4. Remove the steaks from the grill and transfer to them a cutting board. Tent with aluminum foil. 5. Repeat step 3 with the remaining 2 steaks. 6. While the second set of steaks is cooking, assemble the salad by tossing together the lettuce, tomatoes, blue cheese crumbles, and croutons. Top with the avocado slices. 7. Once the second set of steaks has finished cooking, slice all four of the steaks into thin strips, and place on top of the salad. Drizzle with the blue cheese dressing and serve.

Chapter 5 Beef, Pork, and Lamb

Swedish Beef Meatballs

Prep time: 10 minutes | Cook time: 12 minutes | Serves 8

1 pound (454 g) ground beef

1 egg, beaten

2 carrots, shredded

2 bread slices, crumbled

1 small onion, minced

½ teaspoons garlic salt

Pepper and salt, to taste

1 cup tomato sauce

2 cups pasta sauce

1. Add about 2 cups water to the water tray. Press the Power button on the Power Smokeless Grill XL, and set the grill temperature to 390° F (199° C). Allow the grill to preheat for 5 minutes. 2. In a bowl, combine the ground beef, egg, carrots, crumbled bread, onion, garlic salt, pepper and salt. 3. Divide the mixture into equal amounts and shape each one into a small meatball. 4. Once preheated, put them in the grill. Press the Fan button to engage the fan. Close the glass lid and cook for 7 minutes. 5. Transfer the meatballs to an oven-safe dish and top with the tomato sauce and pasta sauce. 6. Set the dish into the grill and allow to cook at 320°F (160ºC) for 5 more minutes. Serve hot.

Vietnamese Pork Chops

Prep time: 15 minutes | Cook time: 12 minutes | Serves 2

1 tablespoon chopped shallot

1 tablespoon chopped garlic

1 tablespoon fish sauce

3 tablespoons lemongrass

1 teaspoon soy sauce

1 tablespoon brown sugar

1 tablespoon olive oil

1 teaspoon ground black pepper

2 pork chops

1. Combine shallot, garlic, fish sauce, lemongrass, soy sauce, brown sugar, olive oil, and pepper in a bowl. Stir to mix well. 2. Put the pork chops in the bowl. Toss to coat well. Place the bowl in the refrigerator to marinate for 2 hours. 3. Add about 2 cups water to the water tray. Press the Power button on the Power Smokeless Grill XL, and set the grill temperature to 390° F (199° C). Allow the grill to preheat for 5 minutes. 4. Once preheated, remove the pork chops from the bowl and discard the marinade. Transfer the chops into the grill. 5. Press the Fan button to engage the fan. Close the glass lid and cook for 12 minutes or until lightly browned. Flip the pork chops halfway through the cooking time. 6. Remove the pork chops from the grill and serve hot.

Smoked Beef

Prep time: 10 minutes | Cook time: 45 minutes | Serves 8

2 pounds (907 g) roast beef, at room temperature

2 tablespoons extra-virgin olive oil

1 teaspoon sea salt flakes

1 teaspoon ground black pepper

1 teaspoon smoked paprika

Few dashes of liquid smoke

2 jalapeño peppers, thinly sliced

1. Add about 2 cups water to the water tray. Press the Power button on the Power Smokeless Grill XL, and set the grill temperature to 320° F (160° C). Allow the grill to preheat for 5 minutes. 2. With kitchen towels, pat the beef dry. 3. Massage the extra-virgin olive oil, salt, black pepper, and paprika into the meat. Cover with liquid smoke. 4. Once preheated, put the beef over the grill plate. Press the Fan button to engage the fan. Close the glass lid and grill for 30 minutes. Flip the roast over and allow to cook for another 15 minutes. 5. When cooked through, serve topped with sliced jalapeños.

Smoky Paprika Pork and Vegetable Kabobs

Prep time: 25 minutes | Cook time: 15 minutes | Serves 4

1 pound (454 g) pork tenderloin, cubed

1 teaspoon smoked paprika

Salt and ground black pepper, to taste

1 green bell pepper, cut into chunks

1 zucchini, cut into chunks

1 red onion, sliced

1 tablespoon oregano

Cooking spray

Special Equipment:

Small bamboo skewers, soaked in water for 20 minutes to keep them from burning while cooking

1. Spritz the grill plate with cooking spray. 2. Add about 2 cups water to the water tray. Press the Power button on the Power Smokeless Grill XL, and set the grill temperature to 350°F (177°C). Allow the grill to preheat for 5 minutes. 3. Add the pork to a bowl and season with the smoked paprika, salt and black pepper. Thread the seasoned pork cubes and vegetables alternately onto the soaked skewers. 4. Once preheated, arrange the skewers on the prepared grill plate and spray with cooking spray. 5. Press the Fan button to engage the fan. Close the glass lid and cook for 15 minutes, or until the pork is well browned and the vegetables are tender, flipping once halfway through. 6. Transfer the skewers to the serving dishes and sprinkle with oregano. Serve hot.

Bacon-Wrapped Sausage with Tomato Relish

Prep time: 1 hour 15 minutes | Cook time: 32 minutes | Serves 4

8 pork sausages

8 bacon strips

Relish:

8 large tomatoes, chopped

1 small onion, peeled

1 clove garlic, peeled

1 tablespoon white wine vinegar

3 tablespoons chopped parsley

1 teaspoon smoked paprika

2 tablespoons sugar

Salt and ground black pepper, to taste

1. Purée the tomatoes, onion, and garlic in a food processor until well mixed and smooth. 2. Pour the purée in a saucepan and drizzle with white wine vinegar. Sprinkle with salt and ground black pepper. Simmer over medium heat for 10 minutes. 3. Add the parsley, paprika, and sugar to the saucepan and cook for 10 more minutes or until it has a thick consistency. Keep stirring during the cooking. Refrigerate for an hour to chill. 4. Add about 2 cups water to the water tray. Press the Power button on the Power Smokeless Grill XL, and set the grill temperature to 350°F (177°C). Allow the grill to preheat for 5 minutes. 5. Once preheated, wrap the sausage with bacon strips and secure with toothpicks, then place them in the grill. 6. Press the Fan button to engage the fan. Close the glass lid and cook for 12 minutes or until the bacon is crispy and browned. Flip the bacon-wrapped sausage halfway through. 7. Transfer the bacon-wrapped sausage on a plate and baste with the relish or just serve with the relish alongside.

Beef and Vegetable Cubes

Prep time: 15 minutes | Cook time: 17 minutes | Serves 4

2 tablespoons olive oil

1 tablespoon apple cider vinegar

1 teaspoon fine sea salt

½ teaspoons ground black pepper

1 teaspoon shallot powder

¾ teaspoon smoked cayenne pepper

½ teaspoons garlic powder

¼ teaspoon ground cumin

1 pound (454 g) top round steak, cut into cubes

4 ounces (113 g) broccoli, cut into florets

4 ounces (113 g) mushrooms, sliced

1 teaspoon dried basil

1 teaspoon celery seeds

1. Massage the olive oil, vinegar, salt, black pepper, shallot powder, cayenne pepper, garlic powder, and cumin into the cubed steak, ensuring to coat each piece evenly. 2. Allow to marinate for a minimum of 3 hours. 3. Add about 2 cups water to the water tray. Press the Power button on the Power Smokeless Grill XL, and set the grill temperature to 350° F (180° C). Allow the grill to preheat for 5 minutes. 4. Once preheated, put the beef cubes on the grill plate. Press the Fan button to engage the fan. Close the glass lid and cook for 12 minutes. 5. When the steak is cooked through, place it in a bowl. 6. Pour in the vegetables. Season them with basil and celery seeds. 7. Increase the temperature of the grill to 390° F (199° C) and cook for 5 to 6 minutes. When the vegetables are hot, serve them with the steak.

Pepperoni and Bell Pepper Pockets

Prep time: 5 minutes | Cook time: 8 minutes | Serves 4

4 bread slices, 1-inch thick

Olive oil, for misting

24 slices pepperoni

1 ounce (28 g) roasted red peppers, drained and patted dry

1 ounce (28 g) Pepper Jack cheese, cut into 4 slices

1. Add about 2 cups water to the water tray. Press the Power button on the Power Smokeless Grill XL, and set the grill temperature to 350° F (180° C). Allow the grill to preheat for 5 minutes. 2. Spray both sides of bread slices with olive oil. 3. Stand slices upright and cut a deep slit in the top to create a pocket (almost to the bottom crust, but not all the way through). 4. Stuff each bread pocket with 6 slices of pepperoni, a large strip of roasted red pepper, and a slice of cheese. 5. Once preheated, put bread pockets in the grill, standing up. Press the Fan button to engage the fan. Close the glass lid and cook for 8 minutes, until filling is heated through and bread is lightly browned. 6. Serve hot.

Cheesy Beef Meatballs

Prep time: 5 minutes | Cook time: 18 minutes | Serves 6

1 pound (454 g) ground beef

½ cup grated Parmesan cheese

1 tablespoon minced garlic

½ cup Mozzarella cheese

1 teaspoon freshly ground pepper

1. Add about 2 cups water to the water tray. Press the Power button on the Power Smokeless Grill XL, and set the grill temperature to 390° F (199° C). Allow the grill to preheat for 5 minutes. 2. In a bowl, mix all the ingredients together. 3. Roll the meat mixture into 5 generous meatballs. Once preheated, transfer to the grill plate. 4. Press the Fan button to engage the fan. Close the glass lid and cook for 18 minutes. 5. Serve immediately.

Pork Sausage with Cauliflower Mash

Prep time: 5 minutes | Cook time: 27 minutes | Serves 6

1 pound (454 g) cauliflower, chopped

6 pork sausages, chopped

½ onion, sliced

3 eggs, beaten

⅓ cup Colby cheese

1 teaspoon cumin powder

½ teaspoon tarragon

½ teaspoon sea salt

½ teaspoon ground black pepper

Cooking spray

1. Add about 2 cups water to the water tray. Press the Power button on the Power Smokeless Grill XL, and set the grill temperature to 350° F (180° C). Allow the grill to preheat for 5 minutes. 2. Spritz a baking pan with cooking spray. 3. In a saucepan over medium heat, boil the cauliflower until tender. Place the boiled cauliflower in a food processor and pulse until puréed. Transfer to a large bowl and combine with remaining ingredients until well blended. 4. Pour the cauliflower and sausage mixture into the baking pan. Once preheated, place the pan directly over the grill plate. Press the Fan button to engage the fan. Close the glass lid and bake for 27 minutes, or until lightly browned. 5. Divide the mixture among six serving dishes and serve warm.

Citrus Carnitas

Prep time: 1 hour 10 minutes | Cook time: 25 minutes | Serves 6

2½ pounds (1.1 kg) boneless country-style pork ribs, cut into 2-inch pieces

3 tablespoons olive brine

1 tablespoon minced fresh oregano leaves

⅓ cup orange juice

1 teaspoon ground cumin

1 tablespoon minced garlic

1 teaspoon salt

1 teaspoon ground black pepper

Cooking spray

1. Combine all the ingredients in a large bowl. Toss to coat the pork ribs well. Wrap the bowl in plastic and refrigerate for at least an hour to marinate. 2. Spritz the grill plate with cooking spray. 3. Add about 2 cups water to the water tray. Press the Power button on the Power Smokeless Grill XL, and set the grill temperature to 390° F (199° C). Allow the grill to preheat for 5 minutes. 4. Once preheated, arrange the marinated pork ribs in a single layer in the grill and spritz with cooking spray. 5. Press the Fan button to engage the fan. Close the glass lid and cook for 25 minutes or until well browned. Flip the ribs halfway through. 6. Serve immediately.

Fast Lamb Satay

Prep time: 5 minutes | Cook time: 8 minutes | Serves 2

¼ teaspoon cumin

1 teaspoon ginger

½ teaspoons nutmeg

Salt and ground black pepper, to taste

2 boneless lamb steaks

Cooking spray

1. Combine the cumin, ginger, nutmeg, salt and pepper in a bowl. 2. Cube the lamb steaks and massage the spice mixture into each one. 3. Leave to marinate for 10 minutes, then transfer onto metal skewers. 4. Add about 2 cups water to the water tray. Press the Power button on the Power Smokeless Grill XL, and set the grill temperature to 390° F (199° C). Allow the grill to preheat for 5 minutes. 5. Once preheated, place the skewers in the grill and spritz with cooking spray. Press the Fan button to engage the fan. Close the glass lid and cook for 8 minutes. 6. Take care when removing them from the grill and serve.

Sausage Ratatouille

Prep time: 10 minutes | Cook time: 25 minutes | Serves 4

4 pork sausages

Ratatouille:

2 zucchinis, sliced

1 eggplant, sliced

15 ounces (425 g) tomatoes, sliced

1 red bell pepper, sliced

1 medium red onion, sliced

1 cup canned butter beans, drained

1 tablespoon balsamic vinegar

2 garlic cloves, minced

1 red chili, chopped

2 tablespoons fresh thyme, chopped

2 tablespoons olive oil

1. Add about 2 cups water to the water tray. Press the Power button on the Power Smokeless Grill XL, and set the grill temperature to 390°F (199°C). Allow the grill to preheat for 5 minutes. 2. Once preheated, place the sausages in the grill. Close the glass lid and cook for 10 minutes or until the sausage is lightly browned. Flip the sausages halfway through. 3. Meanwhile, make the ratatouille: arrange the vegetable slices on the a baking pan alternatively, then add the remaining ingredients on top. 4. Transfer the sausage to a plate. Once preheated, place the pan directly over the grill plate. Press the Fan button to engage the fan. Close the glass lid and bake for 15 minutes or until the vegetables are tender. 5. Serve the ratatouille with the sausage on top.

Spicy Pork with Candy Onions

Prep time: 10 minutes | Cook time: 52 minutes | Serves 4

2 teaspoons sesame oil

1 teaspoon dried sage, crushed

1 teaspoon cayenne pepper

1 rosemary sprig, chopped

1 thyme sprig, chopped

Sea salt and ground black pepper, to taste

2 pounds (907 g) pork leg roast, scored

½ pound (227 g) candy onions, sliced

4 cloves garlic, finely chopped

2 chili peppers, minced

1. Add about 2 cups water to the water tray. Press the Power button on the Power Smokeless Grill XL, and set the grill temperature to 390°F (199°C). Allow the grill to preheat for 5 minutes. 2. In a mixing bowl, combine the sesame oil, sage, cayenne pepper, rosemary, thyme, salt and black pepper until well mixed. In another bowl, place the pork leg and brush with the seasoning mixture. 3. Once preheated, place the seasoned pork leg in a baking pan. Place the pan directly over the grill plate. Press the Fan button to engage the fan. Close the glass lid and cook for 40 minutes, or until lightly browned, flipping halfway through. Add the candy onions, garlic and chili peppers to the pan and cook for another 12 minutes. 4. Transfer the pork leg to a plate. Let cool for 5 minutes and slice. Spread the juices left in the pan over the pork and serve warm with the candy onions.

Homemade Teriyaki Pork Ribs

Prep time: 5 minutes | Cook time: 30 minutes | Serves 4

¼ cup soy sauce

¼ cup honey

1 teaspoon garlic powder

1 teaspoon ground dried ginger

4 (8-ounce / 227-g) boneless country-style pork ribs

Cooking spray

1. Spritz the grill plate with cooking spray. 2. Add about 2 cups water to the water tray. Press the Power button on the Power Smokeless Grill XL, and set the grill temperature to 350°F (177°C). Allow the grill to preheat for 5 minutes. 3. Make the teriyaki sauce: combine the soy sauce, honey, garlic powder, and ginger in a bowl. Stir to mix well. 4. Once preheated, brush the ribs with half of the teriyaki sauce, then arrange the ribs in the grill. Spritz with cooking spray. You may need to work in batches to avoid overcrowding. 5. Press the Fan button to engage the fan. Close the glass lid and cook for 30 minutes or until the internal temperature of the ribs reaches at least 145°F (63°C). Brush the ribs with remaining teriyaki sauce and flip halfway through. 6. Serve immediately.

Apple-Glazed Pork

Prep time: 15 minutes | Cook time: 19 minutes | Serves 4

1 sliced apple

1 small onion, sliced

2 tablespoons apple cider vinegar, divided

½ teaspoon thyme

½ teaspoon rosemary

¼ teaspoon brown sugar

3 tablespoons olive oil, divided

¼ teaspoon smoked paprika

4 pork chops

Salt and ground black pepper, to taste

1. Add about 2 cups water to the water tray. Press the Power button on the Power Smokeless Grill XL, and set the grill temperature to 350°F (177°C). Allow the grill to preheat for 5 minutes. 2. Combine the apple slices, onion, 1 tablespoon of vinegar, thyme, rosemary, brown sugar, and 2 tablespoons of olive oil in a baking pan. Stir to mix well. 3. Once preheated, place the pan directly over the grill plate. Press the Fan button to engage the fan. Close the glass lid and bake for 4 minutes. 4. Meanwhile, combine the remaining vinegar and olive oil, and paprika in a large bowl. Sprinkle with salt and ground black pepper. Stir to mix well. Dredge the pork in the mixture and toss to coat well. 5. Remove the baking pan from the grill and put in the pork. Place the pan directly over the grill plate. Close the glass lid and cook for 10 minutes to lightly brown the pork. Flip the pork chops halfway through. 6. Remove the pork from the grill and baste with baked apple mixture on both sides. Put the pork back to the grill and cook for an additional 5 minutes. Flip halfway through. Serve immediately.

Lamb Ribs with Fresh Mint

Prep time: 5 minutes | Cook time: 18 minutes | Serves 4

2 tablespoons mustard

1 pound (454 g) lamb ribs

1 teaspoon rosemary, chopped

Salt and ground black pepper, to taste

¼ cup mint leaves, chopped

1 cup Greek yogurt

1. Add about 2 cups water to the water tray. Press the Power button on the Power Smokeless Grill XL, and set the grill temperature to 350°F (177°C). Allow the grill to preheat for 5 minutes. 2. Use a brush to apply the mustard to the lamb ribs, and season with rosemary, salt, and pepper. Once preheated, transfer to the grill. 3. Press the Fan button to engage the fan. Close the glass lid and cook for 18 minutes. 4. Meanwhile, combine the mint leaves and yogurt in a bowl. 5. Remove the lamb ribs from the grill when cooked and serve with the mint yogurt.

Spaghetti Squash Lasagna

Prep time: 5 minutes | Cook time: 1 hour 15 minutes | Serves 6

2 large spaghetti squash, cooked (about 2¾ pounds / 1.2 kg)

4 pounds (1.8 kg) ground beef

1 (2½-pound / 1.1-kg) large jar Marinara sauce

25 slices Mozzarella cheese

30 ounces whole-milk ricotta cheese

1. Add about 2 cups water to the water tray. Press the Power button on the Power Smokeless Grill XL, and set the grill temperature to 390°F (199°C). Allow the grill to preheat for 5 minutes. 2. Slice the spaghetti squash and place it face down inside a baking pan. Fill with water until covered. 3. Once preheated, place the pan directly over the grill plate. Press the Fan button to engage the fan. Close the glass lid and bake for 45 minutes until skin is soft. 4. Sear the ground beef in a skillet over medium-high heat for 5 minutes or until browned, then add the marinara sauce and heat until warm. Set aside. 5. Scrape the flesh off the cooked squash to resemble strands of spaghetti. 6. Layer the lasagna in a large greased pan in alternating layers of spaghetti squash, beef sauce, Mozzarella, ricotta. Repeat until all the ingredients have been used. 7. Place the pan directly over the grill plate. Close the glass lid and bake for 30 minutes. 8. Serve.

Easy Beef Schnitzel

Prep time: 5 minutes | Cook time: 12 minutes | Serves 1

½ cup friendly bread crumbs

2 tablespoons olive oil

Pepper and salt, to taste

1 egg, beaten

1 thin beef schnitzel

1. Add about 2 cups water to the water tray. Press the Power button on the Power Smokeless Grill XL, and set the grill temperature to 350°F (177°C). Allow the grill to preheat for 5 minutes. 2. In a shallow dish, combine the bread crumbs, oil, pepper, and salt. 3. In a second shallow dish, place the beaten egg. 4. Dredge the schnitzel in the egg before rolling it in the bread crumbs. 5. Once preheated, put the coated schnitzel in the grill. Press the Fan button to engage the fan. Close the glass lid and cook for 12 minutes. Flip the schnitzel halfway through. 6. Serve immediately.

Chapter 6 Fish and Seafood

Cajun-Style Fish Tacos

Prep time: 5 minutes | Cook time: 10 to 15 minutes | Serves 6

2 teaspoons avocado oil

1 tablespoon Cajun seasoning

4 tilapia fillets

1 (14-ounce / 397-g) package coleslaw mix

12 corn tortillas

2 limes, cut into wedges

1. Line the grill plate with parchment paper. Add about 2 cups water to the water tray. 2. Press the Power button on the Power Smokeless Grill XL, and set the grill temperature to 390°F (199°C). Allow the grill to preheat for 5 minutes. 3. In a medium, shallow bowl, mix the avocado oil and the Cajun seasoning to make a marinade. Add the tilapia fillets and coat evenly. 4. Once preheated, place the fillets in the grill in a single layer, leaving room between each fillet. You may need to cook in batches. 5. Press the Fan button to engage the fan. Close the glass lid and cook for 10 to 15 minutes until the fish is cooked and easily flakes with a fork. 6. Assemble the tacos by placing some of the coleslaw mix in each tortilla. Add ⅓ of a tilapia fillet to each tortilla. Squeeze some lime juice over the top of each taco and serve.

Garlic-Lemon Tilapia

Prep time: 5 minutes | Cook time: 10 to 15 minutes | Serves 4

1 tablespoon lemon juice

1 tablespoon olive oil

1 teaspoon minced garlic

½ teaspoon chili powder

4 (6-ounce / 170-g) tilapia fillets

1. Line the grill plate with parchment paper. 2. Add about 2 cups water to the water tray. Press the Power button on the Power Smokeless Grill XL, and set the grill temperature to 390°F (199°C). Allow the grill to preheat for 5 minutes. 3. In a large, shallow bowl, mix together the lemon juice, olive oil, garlic, and chili powder to make a marinade. Place the tilapia fillets in the bowl and coat evenly. 4. Once preheated, place the fillets in the grill in a single layer, leaving space between each fillet. You may need to cook in more than one batch. 5. Press the Fan button to engage the fan. Close the glass lid and cook for 10 to 15 minutes until the fish is cooked and flakes easily with a fork. 6. Serve hot.

Green Curry Shrimp

Prep time: 15 minutes | Cook time: 5 minutes | Serves 4

1 to 2 tablespoons Thai green curry paste

2 tablespoons coconut oil, melted

1 tablespoon half-and-half or coconut milk

1 teaspoon fish sauce

1 teaspoon soy sauce

1 teaspoon minced fresh ginger

1 clove garlic, minced

1 pound (454 g) jumbo raw shrimp, peeled and deveined

¼ cup chopped fresh Thai basil or sweet basil

¼ cup chopped fresh cilantro

1. In a baking pan, combine the curry paste, coconut oil, half-and-half, fish sauce, soy sauce, ginger, and garlic. Whisk until well combined. 2. Add the shrimp and toss until well coated. Marinate at room temperature for 15 to 30 minutes. 3. Add about 2 cups water to the water tray. Press the Power button on the Power Smokeless Grill XL, and set the grill temperature to 390°F (199°C). Allow the grill to preheat for 5 minutes. 4. Once preheated, place the pan directly over the grill plate. Press the Fan button to engage the fan. Close the glass lid and cook for 5 minutes, stirring halfway through the cooking time. 5. Transfer the shrimp to a serving bowl or platter. Garnish with the basil and cilantro. Serve immediately.

Crispy Cod Cakes with Salad Greens

Prep time: 15 minutes | Cook time: 12 minutes | Serves 4

1 pound (454 g) cod fillets, cut into chunks

⅓ cup packed fresh basil leaves

3 cloves garlic, crushed

½ teaspoon smoked paprika

¼ teaspoon salt

¼ teaspoon pepper

1 large egg, beaten

1 cup panko bread crumbs

Cooking spray

Salad greens, for serving

1. In a food processor, pulse cod, basil, garlic, smoked paprika, salt, and pepper until cod is finely chopped, stirring occasionally. Form into 8 patties, about 2 inches in diameter. Dip each first into the egg, then into the panko, patting to adhere. Spray with oil on one side. 2. Add about 2 cups water to the water tray. Press the Power button on the Power Smokeless Grill XL, and set the grill temperature to 390°F (199°C). Allow the grill to preheat for 5 minutes. 3. Once preheated, working in batches, place half the cakes in the grill, oil-side down; spray with oil. Press the Fan button to engage the fan. Close the glass lid and cook for 12 minutes, until golden brown and cooked through. 4. Serve cod cakes with salad greens.

Crispy Crab and Fish Cakes

Prep time: 20 minutes | Cook time: 10 to 12 minutes | Serves 4

8 ounces (227 g) imitation crab meat

4 ounces (113 g) leftover cooked fish (such as cod, pollock, or haddock)

2 tablespoons minced celery

2 tablespoons minced green onion

2 tablespoons light mayonnaise

1 tablespoon plus 2 teaspoons Worcestershire sauce

¾ cup crushed saltine cracker crumbs

2 teaspoons dried parsley flakes

1 teaspoon prepared yellow mustard

½ teaspoon garlic powder

½ teaspoon dried dill weed, crushed

½ teaspoon Old Bay seasoning

½ cup panko bread crumbs

Cooking spray

1. Add about 2 cups water to the water tray. Press the Power button on the Power Smokeless Grill XL, and set the grill temperature to 390°F (199°C). Allow the grill to preheat for 5 minutes. 2. Pulse the crab meat and fish in a food processor until finely chopped. 3. Transfer the meat mixture to a large bowl, along with the celery, green onion, mayo, Worcestershire sauce, cracker crumbs, parsley flakes, mustard, garlic powder, dill weed, and Old Bay seasoning. Stir to mix well. 4. Scoop out the meat mixture and form into 8 equal-sized patties with your hands. 5. Place the panko bread crumbs on a plate. Roll the patties in the bread crumbs until they are evenly coated on

both sides. Spritz the patties with cooking spray. 6. Once preheated, put the patties in the grill plate. Press the Fan button to engage the fan. Close the glass lid and bake for 10 to 12 minutes, flipping them halfway through, or until they are golden brown and cooked through. 7. Divide the patties among four plates and serve.

Bacon-Wrapped Scallops

Prep time: 5 minutes | Cook time: 10 minutes | Serves 4

8 (1-ounce / 28-g) sea scallops, cleaned and patted dry

8 slices sugar-free bacon

¼ teaspoon salt

¼ teaspoon ground black pepper

1. Add about 2 cups water to the water tray. 2. Press the Power button on the Power Smokeless Grill XL, and set the grill temperature to 350°F (180°C). Allow the grill to preheat for 5 minutes. 3. Wrap each scallop in 1 slice bacon and secure with a toothpick. Sprinkle with salt and pepper. 4. Once preheated, place scallops into the grill. Press the Fan button to engage the fan. Close the glass lid and cook for 10 to 12 minutes. Scallops will be opaque and firm, and have an internal temperature of 135°F (57°C) when done. Serve warm.

Crab Ratatouille with Eggplant and Tomatoes

Prep time: 15 minutes | Cook time: 11 to 14 minutes | Serves 4

1½ cups peeled and cubed eggplant

2 large tomatoes, chopped

1 red bell pepper, chopped

1 onion, chopped

1 tablespoon olive oil

½ teaspoon dried basil

½ teaspoon dried thyme

Pinch salt

Freshly ground black pepper, to taste

1½ cups cooked crab meat

1. Add about 2 cups water to the water tray. Press the Power button on the Power Smokeless Grill XL, and set the grill temperature to 390°F (199°C). Allow the grill to preheat for 5 minutes. 2. Press the Fan button to engage the fan. 3. Once preheated, stir together the eggplant, tomatoes, bell pepper, onion, olive oil, basil and thyme in the grill. Season with salt and pepper. 4. Close the glass lid and grill for 9 minutes. 5. Add the crab meat and stir well and cook for another 2 to 5 minutes, or until the vegetables are softened and the ratatouille is bubbling. 6. Serve warm.

Air-Fried Scallops

Prep time: 10 minutes | Cook time: 12 minutes | Serves 2

⅓ cup shallots, chopped

1½ tablespoons olive oil

1½ tablespoons coconut aminos

1 tablespoon Mediterranean seasoning mix

½ tablespoon balsamic vinegar

½ teaspoon ginger, grated

1 clove garlic, chopped

1 pound (454 g) scallops, cleaned

Cooking spray

Belgian endive, for garnish

1. Place all the ingredients except the scallops and Belgian endive in a small skillet over medium heat and stir to combine. Let this mixture simmer for about 2 minutes. 2. Remove the mixture from the skillet to a large bowl and set aside to cool. 3. Add the scallops, coating them all over, then transfer to the refrigerator to marinate for at least 2 hours. 4. Add about 2 cups water to the water tray. Press the Power button on the Power Smokeless Grill XL, and set the grill temperature to 350°F (180°C). Allow the grill to preheat for 5 minutes. 5. Once preheated, arrange the scallops in the grill plate in a single layer and spray with cooking spray. 6. Press the Fan button to engage the fan. Close the glass lid and cook for 10 minutes, flipping the scallops halfway through, or until the scallops are tender and opaque. 7. Serve garnished with the Belgian endive.

Roasted Cod with Sesame Seeds

Prep time: 5 minutes | Cook time: 7 to 9 minutes | Makes 1 fillet

1 tablespoon reduced-sodium soy sauce

2 teaspoons honey

Cooking spray

6 ounces (170 g) fresh cod fillet

1 teaspoon sesame seeds

1. Add about 2 cups water to the water tray. Press the Power button on the Power Smokeless Grill XL, and set the grill temperature to 350°F (180°C). Allow the grill to preheat for 5 minutes. 2. In a small bowl, combine the soy sauce and honey. 3. Once preheated, spray the grill plate with cooking spray, then place the cod in the grill, brush with the soy mixture, and sprinkle sesame seeds on top. 4. Press the Fan button to engage the fan. Close the glass lid and grill for 7 to 9 minutes, or until opaque. 5. Remove the fish and allow to cool on a wire rack for 5 minutes before serving.

Fired Shrimp with Mayonnaise Sauce

Prep time: 5 minutes | Cook time: 7 minutes | Serves 4

Shrimp:

12 jumbo shrimp

½ teaspoon garlic salt

¼ teaspoon freshly cracked mixed peppercorns

Sauce:

4 tablespoons mayonnaise

1 teaspoon grated lemon rind

1 teaspoon Dijon mustard

1 teaspoon chipotle powder

½ teaspoon cumin powder

1. Add about 2 cups water to the water tray. Press the Power button on the Power Smokeless Grill XL, and set the grill temperature to 390°F (199°C). Allow the grill to preheat for 5 minutes. 2. In a medium bowl, season the shrimp with garlic salt and cracked mixed peppercorns. 3. Once preheated, place the shrimp in the grill plate. Press the Fan button to engage the fan. Close the glass lid and cook for 5 minutes. Flip the shrimp and cook for another 2 minutes until they are pink and no longer opaque. 4. Meanwhile, stir together all the ingredients for the sauce in a small bowl until well mixed. 5. Remove the shrimp from the grill and serve alongside the sauce.

Chapter 7 Desserts

Chocolate Coconut Brownies

Prep time: 15 minutes | Cook time: 15 minutes | Serves 8

½ cup coconut oil

2 ounces (57 g) dark chocolate

1 cup sugar

2½ tablespoons water

4 whisked eggs

¼ teaspoon ground cinnamon

½ teaspoons ground anise star

¼ teaspoon coconut extract

½ teaspoons vanilla extract

1 tablespoon honey

½ cup flour

½ cup desiccated coconut

Sugar, for dusting

1. Add about 2 cups water to the water tray. Press the Power button on the Power Smokeless Grill XL, and set the grill temperature to 350°F (180°C). Allow the grill to preheat for 5 minutes. 2. Melt the coconut oil and dark chocolate in the microwave. 3. Combine with the sugar, water, eggs, cinnamon, anise, coconut extract, vanilla, and honey in a large bowl. 4. Stir in the flour and desiccated coconut. Incorporate everything well. 5. Lightly grease a baking pan with butter. Transfer the mixture to the pan. 6. Once preheated, place the pan directly over the grill plate. Press the Fan button to engage the fan. Close the glass lid and bake for 15 minutes. 7. Remove from the grill and allow to

cool slightly. 8. Take care when taking it out of the baking pan. Slice it into squares. 9. Dust with sugar before serving.

Chia Pudding

Prep time: 5 minutes | Cook time: 4 minutes | Serves 2

1 cup chia seeds

1 cup unsweetened coconut milk

1 teaspoon liquid stevia

1 tablespoon coconut oil

1 teaspoon butter, melted

1. Add about 2 cups water to the water tray. Press the Power button on the Power Smokeless Grill XL, and set the grill temperature to 350°F (180°C). Allow the grill to preheat for 5 minutes. 2. Mix together the chia seeds, coconut milk, and stevia in a large bowl. Add the coconut oil and melted butter and stir until well blended. 3. Divide the mixture evenly between the ramekins, filling only about ⅔ of the way. Once preheated, transfer to the grill. 4. Press the Fan button to engage the fan. Close the glass lid and bake for 4 minutes. 5. Allow to cool for 5 minutes and serve warm.

Chocolate and Peanut Butter Lava Cupcakes

Prep time: 10 minutes | Cook time: 10 to 13 minutes | Serves 8

Nonstick baking spray with flour

1⅓ cups chocolate cake mix

1 egg

1 egg yolk

¼ cup safflower oil

¼ cup hot water

⅓ cup sour cream

3 tablespoons peanut butter

1 tablespoon powdered sugar

1. Add about 2 cups water to the water tray. Press the Power button on the Power Smokeless Grill XL, and set the grill temperature to 350°F (177°C). Allow the grill to preheat for 5 minutes. 2. Double up 16 foil muffin cups to make 8 cups. Spray each lightly with nonstick spray; set aside. 3. In a medium bowl, combine the cake mix, egg, egg yolk, safflower oil, water, and sour cream, and beat until combined. 4. In a small bowl, combine the peanut butter and powdered sugar and mix well. Form this mixture into 8 balls. 5. Spoon about ¼ cup of the chocolate batter into each muffin cup and top with a peanut butter ball. Spoon remaining batter on top of the peanut butter balls to cover them. 6. Once preheated, arrange the cups over the grill plate, leaving some space between each. Place the pan directly over the grill plate. Press the Fan button to engage the fan. Close the glass lid and bake for 10 to 13 minutes or until the tops look dry and set. 7. Let the cupcakes cool for about 10 minutes, then serve warm.

Ultimate Skillet Brownies

Prep time: 15 minutes | Cook time: 40 minutes | Serves 6

½ cup all-purpose flour

¼ cup unsweetened cocoa powder

¾ teaspoon sea salt

2 large eggs

1 tablespoon water

½ cup granulated sugar

½ cup dark brown sugar

1 tablespoon vanilla extract

8 ounces (227 g) semisweet chocolate chips, melted

¾ cup unsalted butter, melted

Nonstick cooking spray

1. In a medium bowl, whisk together the flour, cocoa powder, and salt. 2. In a large bowl, whisk together the eggs, water, sugar, brown sugar, and vanilla until smooth. 3. In a microwave-safe bowl, melt the chocolate in the microwave. In a separate microwave-safe bowl, melt the butter. 4. In a separate medium bowl, stir together the chocolate and butter until evenly combined. Whisk into the egg mixture. Then slowly add the dry ingredients, stirring just until incorporated. 5. Add about 2 cups water to the water tray. Press the Power button on the Power Smokeless Grill XL, and set the grill temperature to 350°F (177°C). Allow the grill to preheat for 5 minutes. 6. Meanwhile, lightly grease the baking pan with cooking spray. Pour the batter into the pan, spreading evenly. 7. Once preheated, place the pan directly over the grill plate. Press the Fan button to engage the fan. Close the glass lid and bake for 40 minutes. 8. After 40 minutes, check that baking is complete. A wooden toothpick inserted into the center of

the brownies should come out clean.

Oatmeal and Carrot Cookie Cups

Prep time: 10 minutes | Cook time: 8 minutes | Makes 16 cups

3 tablespoons unsalted butter, at room temperature

¼ cup packed brown sugar

1 tablespoon honey

1 egg white

½ teaspoon vanilla extract

⅓ cup finely grated carrot

½ cup quick-cooking oatmeal

⅓ cup whole-wheat pastry flour

½ teaspoon baking soda

¼ cup dried cherries

1. Add about 2 cups water to the water tray. Press the Power button on the Power Smokeless Grill XL, and set the grill temperature to 350°F (177°C). Allow the grill to preheat for 5 minutes. 2. In a medium bowl, beat the butter, brown sugar, and honey until well combined. 3. Add the egg white, vanilla, and carrot. Beat to combine. 4. Stir in the oatmeal, pastry flour, and baking soda. 5. Stir in the dried cherries. 6. Double up 32 mini muffin foil cups to make 16 cups. Fill each with about 4 teaspoons of dough. Once preheated, place the cookie cups directly over the grill plate. 7. Press the Fan button to engage the fan. Close the glass lid and bake for 8 minutes, 8 at a time, or until light golden brown and just set. Serve warm.

Chocolate and Coconut Cake

Prep time: 5 minutes | Cook time: 15 minutes | Serves 6

½ cup unsweetened chocolate, chopped

½ stick butter, at room temperature

1 tablespoon liquid stevia

1½ cups coconut flour

2 eggs, whisked

½ teaspoon vanilla extract

A pinch of fine sea salt

Cooking spray

1. Place the chocolate, butter, and stevia in a microwave-safe bowl. Microwave for about 30 seconds until melted. 2. Let the chocolate mixture cool for 5 to 10 minutes. 3. Add the remaining ingredients to the bowl of chocolate mixture and whisk to incorporate. 4. Add about 2 cups water to the water tray. Press the Power button on the Power Smokeless Grill XL, and set the grill temperature to 320°F (160°C). Allow the grill to preheat for 5 minutes. 5. Lightly spray a baking pan with cooking spray. 6. Scrape the chocolate mixture into the prepared baking pan. 7. Once preheated, place the pan directly over the grill plate. Press the Fan button to engage the fan. Close the glass lid and bake for 15 minutes, or until the top springs back lightly when gently pressed with your fingers. 8. Let the cake cool for 5 minutes and serve.

Lemony Blackberry Crisp

Prep time: 5 minutes | Cook time: 20 minutes | Serves 1

2 tablespoons lemon juice

⅓ cup powdered erythritol

¼ teaspoon xantham gum

2 cup blackberries

1 cup crunchy granola

1. Add about 2 cups water to the water tray. Press the Power button on the Power Smokeless Grill XL, and set the grill temperature to 350°F (177°C). Allow the grill to preheat for 5 minutes. 2. In a bowl, combine the lemon juice, erythritol, xantham gum, and blackberries. Transfer to a round baking pan and cover with aluminum foil. 3. Once preheated, place the pan directly over the grill plate. Press the Fan button to engage the fan. Close the glass lid and bake for 12 minutes. 4. Take care when removing the pan from the grill. Give the blackberries a stir and top with the granola. 5. Return the pan to the grill and grill at 320°F (160°C) for an additional 3 minutes. Serve once the granola has turned brown and enjoy.

Banana and Walnut Cake

Prep time: 10 minutes | Cook time: 25 minutes | Serves 6

1 pound (454 g) bananas, mashed

8 ounces (227 g) flour

6 ounces (170 g) sugar

3.5 ounces (99 g) walnuts, chopped

2.5 ounces (71 g) butter, melted

2 eggs, lightly beaten

¼ teaspoon baking soda

1. Add about 2 cups water to the water tray. Press the Power button on the Power Smokeless Grill XL, and set the grill temperature to 350°F (180°C). Allow the grill to preheat for 5 minutes. 2. In a bowl, combine the sugar, butter, egg, flour, and baking soda with a whisk. Stir in the bananas and walnuts. 3. Transfer the mixture to a greased baking pan. Once preheated, place the pan directly over the grill plate. Press the Fan button to engage the fan. Close the glass lid and bake for 10 minutes. 4. Reduce the temperature to 320°F (160°C) and bake for another 15 minutes. Serve hot.

Pumpkin Pudding

Prep time: 10 minutes | Cook time: 15 minutes | Serves 4

3 cups pumpkin purée

3 tablespoons honey

1 tablespoon ginger

1 tablespoon cinnamon

1 teaspoon clove

1 teaspoon nutmeg

1 cup full-fat cream

2 eggs

1 cup sugar

1. Add about 2 cups water to the water tray. Press the Power button on the Power Smokeless Grill XL, and set the grill temperature to 390°F (199°C). Allow the grill to preheat for 5 minutes. 2. In a bowl, stir all the ingredients together to combine. 3. Scrape the mixture into a greased baking pan. Once preheated, place the pan directly over the grill plate. Press the Fan button to engage the fan. Close the glass lid and bake for 15 minutes. 4. Serve warm.

Lemon Ricotta Cake

Prep time: 5 minutes | Cook time: 25 minutes | Serves 6

17.5 ounces (496 g) ricotta cheese

5.4 ounces (153 g) sugar

3 eggs, beaten

3 tablespoons flour

1 lemon, juiced and zested

2 teaspoons vanilla extract

1. Add about 2 cups water to the water tray. Press the Power button on the Power Smokeless Grill XL, and set the grill temperature to 320°F (160°C). Allow the grill to preheat for 5 minutes. 2. In a large mixing bowl, stir together all the ingredients until the mixture reaches a creamy consistency. 3. Pour the mixture into a baking pan. Once preheated, place the pan directly over the grill plate. 4. Press the Fan button to engage the fan. Close the glass lid and bake for 25 minutes until a toothpick inserted in the center comes out clean. 5. Allow to cool for 10 minutes on a wire rack before serving.

Fresh Blueberry Cobbler

Prep time: 15 minutes | Cook time: 30 minutes | Serves 6

4 cups fresh blueberries

1 teaspoon grated lemon zest

1 cup sugar, plus 2 tablespoons

1 cup all-purpose flour, plus 2 tablespoons

Juice of 1 lemon

2 teaspoons baking powder

¼ teaspoon salt

6 tablespoons unsalted butter

¾ cup whole milk

⅛ teaspoon ground cinnamon

1. In a medium bowl, combine the blueberries, lemon zest, 2 tablespoons of sugar, 2 tablespoons of flour, and lemon juice. 2. In a medium bowl, combine the remaining 1 cup of flour and 1 cup of sugar, baking powder, and salt. Cut the butter into the flour mixture until it forms an even crumb texture. Stir in the milk until a dough forms. 3. Add about 2 cups water to the water tray. Press the Power button on the Power Smokeless Grill XL, and set the grill temperature to 350°F (177°C). Allow the grill to preheat for 5 minutes. 4. Meanwhile, pour the blueberry mixture into the baking pan, spreading it evenly across the pan. Gently pour the batter over the blueberry mixture, then sprinkle the cinnamon over the top. 5. Once preheated, place the pan directly over the grill plate. Press the Fan button to engage the fan. Close the glass lid and bake for 30 minutes, until lightly golden. 6. When cooking is complete, serve warm.

Rich Chocolate Cookie

Prep time: 10 minutes | Cook time: 9 minutes | Serves 4

Nonstick baking spray with flour

3 tablespoons softened butter

⅓ cup plus 1 tablespoon brown sugar

1 egg yolk

½ cup flour

2 tablespoons ground white chocolate

¼ teaspoon baking soda

½ teaspoon vanilla

¾ cup chocolate chips

1. Add about 2 cups water to the water tray. Press the Power button on the Power Smokeless Grill XL, and set the grill temperature to 350°F (177°C). Allow the grill to preheat for 5 minutes. 2. In a medium bowl, beat the butter and brown sugar together until fluffy. Stir in the egg yolk. 3. Add the flour, white chocolate, baking soda, and vanilla, and mix well. Stir in the chocolate chips. 4. Line a baking pan with parchment paper. Spray the parchment paper with nonstick baking spray with flour. 5. Spread the batter into the prepared pan, leaving a ½-inch border on all sides. 6. Once preheated, place the pan directly over the grill plate. Press the Fan button to engage the fan. Close the glass lid and bake for 9 minutes or until the cookie is light brown and just barely set. 7. Remove the pan from the grill and let cool for 10 minutes. Remove the cookie from the pan, remove the parchment paper, and let cool on a wire rack. 8. Serve immediately.

Classic Pound Cake

Prep time: 5 minutes | Cook time: 30 minutes | Serves 8

1 stick butter, at room temperature

1 cup Swerve

4 eggs

1½ cups coconut flour

½ cup buttermilk

½ teaspoon baking soda

½ teaspoon baking powder

¼ teaspoon salt

1 teaspoon vanilla essence

A pinch of ground star anise

A pinch of freshly grated nutmeg

Cooking spray

1. Add about 2 cups water to the water tray. Press the Power button on the Power Smokeless Grill XL, and set the grill temperature to 320°F (160°C). Allow the grill to preheat for 5 minutes. 2. Spray a baking pan with cooking spray. 3. With an electric mixer or hand mixer, beat the butter and Swerve until creamy. One at a time, mix in the eggs and whisk until fluffy. Add the remaining ingredients and stir to combine. 4. Transfer the batter to the prepared baking pan. Once preheated, place the pan directly over the grill plate. Press the Fan button to engage the fan. Close the glass lid and bake for 30 minutes until the center of the cake is springy. Rotate the pan halfway through the cooking time. 5. Allow the cake to cool in the pan for 10 minutes before removing and serving.

Peanut Butter-Chocolate Bread Pudding

Prep time: 10 minutes | Cook time: 10 to 12 minutes | Serves 8

1 egg

1 egg yolk

¾ cup chocolate milk

3 tablespoons brown sugar

3 tablespoons peanut butter

2 tablespoons cocoa powder

1 teaspoon vanilla

5 slices firm white bread, cubed

Nonstick cooking spray

1. Add about 2 cups water to the water tray. Press the Power button on the Power Smokeless Grill XL, and set the grill temperature to 320°F (160°C). Allow the grill to preheat for 5 minutes. 2. Spritz a baking pan with nonstick cooking spray. 3. Whisk together the egg, egg yolk, chocolate milk, brown sugar, peanut butter, cocoa powder, and vanilla until well combined. 4. Fold in the bread cubes and stir to mix well. Allow the bread soak for 10 minutes. 5. When ready, transfer the egg mixture to the prepared baking pan. 6. Once preheated, place the pan directly over the grill plate. Press the Fan button to engage the fan. Close the glass lid and bake for 10 to 12 minutes, or until the pudding is just firm to the touch. 7. Serve at room temperature.

Chapter 8 Vegetarian Mains

Italian Baked Tofu

Prep time: 5 minutes | Cook time: 10 minutes | Serves 2

1 tablespoon soy sauce

1 tablespoon water

⅓ teaspoon garlic powder

⅓ teaspoon onion powder

⅓ teaspoon dried oregano

⅓ teaspoon dried basil

Black pepper, to taste

6 ounces (170 g) extra firm tofu, pressed and cubed

1. In a large mixing bowl, whisk together the soy sauce, water, garlic powder, onion powder, oregano, basil, and black pepper. Add the tofu cubes, stirring to coat, and let them marinate for 10 minutes. 2. Add about 2 cups water to the water tray. Press the Power button on the Power Smokeless Grill XL, and set the grill temperature to 390°F (199°C). Allow the grill to preheat for 5 minutes. 3. Arrange the tofu in the baking pan. Once preheated, place the pan directly over the grill plate. Press the Fan button to engage the fan. Close the glass lid and bake for 10 minutes until crisp. Flip the tofu halfway through the cooking time. 4. Remove from the grill to a plate and serve.

Rosemary Roasted Squash with Cheese

Prep time: 5 minutes | Cook time: 20 minutes | Serves 2

1 pound (454 g) butternut squash, cut into wedges

2 tablespoons olive oil

1 tablespoon dried rosemary

Salt, to salt

1 cup crumbled goat cheese

1 tablespoon maple syrup

1. Add about 2 cups water to the water tray. Press the Power button on the Power Smokeless Grill XL, and set the grill temperature to 350°F (177°C). Allow the grill to preheat for 5 minutes. 2. Toss the squash wedges with the olive oil, rosemary, and salt in a large bowl until well coated. 3. Once preheated, transfer the squash wedges to the grill plate, spreading them out in as even a layer as possible. 4. Press the Fan button to engage the fan. Close the glass lid and grill for 10 minutes. Flip the squash and roast for another 10 minutes until golden brown. 5. Sprinkle the goat cheese on top and serve drizzled with the maple syrup.

Simple Ratatouille

Prep time: 15 minutes | Cook time: 16 minutes | Serves 2

2 Roma tomatoes, thinly sliced

1 zucchini, thinly sliced

2 yellow bell peppers, sliced

2 garlic cloves, minced

2 tablespoons olive oil

2 tablespoons herbes de Provence

1 tablespoon vinegar

Salt and black pepper, to taste

1. Add about 2 cups water to the water tray. Press the Power button on the Power Smokeless Grill XL, and set the grill temperature to 390°F (199°C). Allow the grill to preheat for 5 minutes. 2. Place the tomatoes, zucchini, bell peppers, garlic, olive oil, herbes de Provence, and vinegar in a large bowl and toss until the vegetables are evenly coated. Sprinkle with salt and pepper and toss again. Once preheated, pour the vegetable mixture into the pot. 3. Press the Fan button to engage the fan. Close the glass lid and grill for 8 minutes. Stir and continue roasting for 8 minutes until tender. 4. Let the vegetable mixture stand for 5 minutes in the grill before removing and serving.

Potatoes with Zucchinis

Prep time: 10 minutes | Cook time: 45 minutes | Serves 4

2 potatoes, peeled and cubed

4 carrots, cut into chunks

1 head broccoli, cut into florets

4 zucchinis, sliced thickly

Salt and ground black pepper, to taste

¼ cup olive oil

1 tablespoon dry onion powder

1. Add about 2 cups water to the water tray. Press the Power button on the Power Smokeless Grill XL, and set the grill temperature to 390°F (199°C). Allow the grill to preheat for 5 minutes. 2. In a baking pan, add all the ingredients and combine well. 3. Once preheated, place the pan directly over the grill plate. Press the Fan button to engage the fan. Close the glass lid and bake for 45 minutes, ensuring the vegetables are soft and the sides have browned before serving.

Mascarpone Mushrooms

Prep time: 10 minutes | Cook time: 15 minutes | Serves 4

Vegetable oil spray

4 cups sliced mushrooms

1 medium yellow onion, chopped

2 cloves garlic, minced

¼ cup heavy whipping cream or half-and-half

8 ounces (227 g) mascarpone cheese

1 teaspoon dried thyme

1 teaspoon kosher salt

1 teaspoon black pepper

½ teaspoon red pepper flakes

4 cups cooked konjac noodles, for serving

½ cup grated Parmesan cheese

1. Add about 2 cups water to the water tray. Press the Power button on the Power Smokeless Grill XL, and set the grill temperature to 350°F (177°C). Allow the grill to preheat for 5 minutes. 2. Spray a heatproof pan with vegetable oil spray. 3. In a medium bowl, combine the mushrooms, onion, garlic, cream, mascarpone, thyme, salt, black pepper, and red pepper flakes. Stir to combine. Transfer the mixture to the prepared pan. 4. Once preheated, place the pan directly over the grill plate. Press the Fan button to engage the fan. Close the glass lid and bake for 15 minutes, stirring halfway through the baking time. 5. Divide the pasta among four shallow bowls. Spoon the mushroom mixture evenly over the pasta. Sprinkle with Parmesan cheese and serve.

Spicy Cauliflower Roast

Prep time: 15 minutes | Cook time: 20 minutes | Serves 4

Cauliflower:

5 cups cauliflower florets

3 tablespoons vegetable oil

½ teaspoon ground cumin

½ teaspoon ground coriander

½ teaspoon kosher salt

Sauce:

½ cup Greek yogurt or sour cream

¼ cup chopped fresh cilantro

1 jalapeño, coarsely chopped

4 cloves garlic, peeled

½ teaspoon kosher salt

2 tablespoons water

1. Add about 2 cups water to the water tray. Press the Power button on the Power Smokeless Grill XL, and set the grill temperature to 390°F (199°C). Allow the grill to preheat for 5 minutes. 2. In a large bowl, combine the cauliflower, oil, cumin, coriander, and salt. Toss to coat. 3. Once preheated, put the cauliflower in the grill. Press the Fan button to engage the fan. Close the glass lid and grill for 20 minutes, stirring halfway through the cooking time. 4. Meanwhile, in a blender, combine the yogurt, cilantro, jalapeño, garlic, and salt. Blend, adding the water as needed to keep the blades moving and to thin the sauce. 5. At the end of cooking time, transfer the cauliflower to a large serving bowl. Pour the sauce over and toss gently to coat. Serve immediately.

Sesame-Thyme Whole Maitake Mushrooms

Prep time: 5 minutes | Cook time: 15 minutes | Serves 2

1 tablespoon soy sauce

2 teaspoons toasted sesame oil

3 teaspoons vegetable oil, divided

1 garlic clove, minced

7 ounces (198 g) maitake (hen of the woods) mushrooms

½ teaspoon flaky sea salt

½ teaspoon sesame seeds

½ teaspoon finely chopped fresh thyme leaves

1. Add about 2 cups water to the water tray. Press the Power button on the Power Smokeless Grill XL, and set the grill temperature to 320°F (160°C). Allow the grill to preheat for 5 minutes. 2. Whisk together the soy sauce, sesame oil, 1 teaspoon of vegetable oil, and garlic in a small bowl. 3. Once preheated, arrange the mushrooms in the grill in a single layer. Drizzle the soy sauce mixture over the mushrooms. Press the Fan button to engage the fan. Close the glass lid and grill for 10 minutes. 4. Flip the mushrooms and sprinkle the sea salt, sesame seeds, and thyme leaves on top. Drizzle the remaining 2 teaspoons of vegetable oil all over. Cook for an additional 5 minutes. 5. Remove the mushrooms from the grill to a plate and serve hot.

Conclusion

The Power XL Smokeless Grill is an efficient grilling appliance for people like me who enjoy grilling indoor. It's smoke-free, compact, and comes with unique parts and accessories that make it perform its job excellently. In this book, I discussed the unique features of the Power XL Smokeless Grill in detail. I also explained the numerous advantages I enjoyed with the Power XL Smokeless grill and provided tips and hints on using your Power XL Smokeless Grill in the best way possible. I'm certain you will be able to make the most of your Power XL Smokeless Grill by inculcating the knowledge you've garnered while reading this book. Good luck!

Appendix 1 Measurement Conversion Chart

MEASUREMENT CONVERSION CHART

VOLUME EQUIVALENTS(DRY)

US STANDARD	METRIC (APPROXIMATE)
1/8 teaspoon	0.5 mL
1/4 teaspoon	1 mL
1/2 teaspoon	2 mL
3/4 teaspoon	4 mL
1 teaspoon	5 mL
1 tablespoon	15 mL
1/4 cup	59 mL
1/2 cup	118 mL
3/4 cup	177 mL
1 cup	235 mL
2 cups	475 mL
3 cups	700 mL
4 cups	1 L

WEIGHT EQUIVALENTS

US STANDARD	METRIC (APPROXIMATE)
1 ounce	28 g
2 ounces	57 g
5 ounces	142 g
10 ounces	284 g
15 ounces	425 g
16 ounces (1 pound)	455 g
1.5 pounds	680 g
2 pounds	907 g

VOLUME EQUIVALENTS(LIQUID)

US STANDARD	US STANDARD (OUNCES)	METRIC (APPROXIMATE)
2 tablespoons	1 fl.oz.	30 mL
1/4 cup	2 fl.oz.	60 mL
1/2 cup	4 fl.oz.	120 mL
1 cup	8 fl.oz.	240 mL
1 1/2 cup	12 fl.oz.	355 mL
2 cups or 1 pint	16 fl.oz.	475 mL
4 cups or 1 quart	32 fl.oz.	1 L
1 gallon	128 fl.oz.	4 L

TEMPERATURES EQUIVALENTS

FAHRENHEIT(F)	CELSIUS(C) (APPROXIMATE)
225 °F	107 °C
250 °F	120 °C
275 °F	135 °C
300 °F	150 °C
325 °F	160 °C
350 °F	180 °C
375 °F	190 °C
400 °F	205 °C
425 °F	220 °C
450 °F	235 °C
475 °F	245 °C
500 °F	260 °C

Cooking Chart

Food Item	Time	Internal Temperature	It's Done When
Fish	12-15 mins.(1-in.thick)	155°F	Opaque/Flaky Texture
Shrimp	2-4 mins.(per side)	155°F	Opaque & Red Edges
Chicken Drumsticks	30-45 mins.	176°F	Juice Runs Clear
Chicken Wings	20-25 mins	176°F	Juice Runs Clear
Kabobs	12-15 mins.	-	Your Preference
Steak	3-9 mins.(per side)	140°F-165°F	Your Preference
Pork Chops	20-25 mins.	160°F	No Pink Meat
Burgers	10-15 mins.	160°F	Your Preference
Sausages	15-25 mins.	160°F	No Pink Meat
Bacon	1-2 mins.(per side)	NA	Crispy

Made in the USA
Las Vegas, NV
17 September 2023

77733570R00057